W9-BLL-836

A12900 383927

ILLINOIS CENTRAL COLLEGE
PS3515.0924B5
STACKS
The blue garden.

A12900 383927

PS
35 15
.O 924
B5

Howes, Bar

The blue garden.

WITHDRAWN

Illinois Central College
Learning Resources Center

THE BLUE GARDEN

THE WESLEYAN POETRY PROGRAM: VOLUME 62

The Blue Garden

BY

BARBARA HOWES

Wesleyan University Press

Middletown, Connecticut

48044

ILLINOIS CENTRAL COLLEGE
LEARNING RESOURCES CENTER

Copyright © 1966, 1967, 1968, 1969, 1970, 1971, 1972 by Barbara Howes

PS
3515
.0924
B5

Most of these poems have previously appeared elsewhere. For permission to reprint, and for the assignment of copyrights, thanks are due to the editors and publishers of the following periodicals:

American Scholar, Antaeus, The Atlantic, Berkshire Review, BIM, Caribbean Review, New American Review, New England Galaxy, The New York Times, Poetry Miscellany, Saturday Review, Southern Review, Stand, Sumac, Virginia Quarterly Review, and *Yale Review.*

"For an Old Friend," "A Letter from Little Tobago," and *"Voyage autour de ma Chambre"* (originally titled "The Harkness Pavilion") were first published in *The New Yorker.*

"A Drachma for Myself" and "Ouroborus" initially appeared in *Poetry.*

Library of Congress Cataloging in Publication Data

Howes, Barbara.
    The blue garden.

    (The Wesleyan poetry program, v. 62)
    I. Title.
PS3515.0924B5   811'.5'4   72-3697
    ISBN 0-8195-2062-4
    ISBN 0-8195-1062-9 (pbk.)

Manufactured in the United States of America

First Edition

for David
and for Gregory

Contents

AWAY

Returning to Store Bay   11
A Letter from Little Tobago   12
Voyage autour de ma Chambre   14
Luke, Captive   15
Wild Geese Flying   17
The Ostrich Tree—The Palm Bird   18
Guests   19
Monkey Difference   20
The Lonely Pipefish   21
Millefleurs   23
Gold *Beyond* Gold   25
Evening: Crown Point   27
Crystal-clear—Diamond-bright   28
Mercedes   29
Sweet Sleep   31
The Cold Stones of the Moon   32
At Mrs. Alefounder's   33
On Buccoo Reef   35

AT HOME

The Blue Garden   39

Otis	41
Adam Breathing	43
Elm Burning	44
At 79th and Park	45
For John	46
First Frost	48
January 26, '71	49
For Mother—A Log	50
Best of Show	51
Focus	53
Threesquare at the Landfill	55
Talking to Animals	56
Shell	58
August	59
Notes for a Foghorn	60
Ouroborus	61
For an Old Friend	62
Jim	63
Still-life: New England	65
A Drachma for Myself	67
Cardinal	69

AWAY

Returning to Store Bay

Coming back to this generous island —
Shore, harbor, beach —
Is to leave behind images blown
Like cats through a shadow alley,
    And the feel of cement in the teeth . . .

Returning to Store Bay
One comes back to the circular sound
Of wind whacking the scrolled
Water, the vast contest
    Of undertow and surf;

To the savage ironing
Of breezes, rolling on out, stropping,
Whaling, pulling back in, the water
Huge in some artisan hand;
    Surf and wind are round.

— In a ferryslip, wings
Of brown paper from a subway
Kiosk play hopscotch, stretch out
In gutters of that town whose
    Sidewalks abrade the throat. —

Coming back to this bay
Is to meet again the guffawing
Ocean, is to dance, dimensional,
Hewed out by wind, in the round,
    Alive in the muscular sea.

A Letter from Little Tobago

This feeling of being alone,
    Visiting all these birds who live here —
    Who are in some way our hosts —
    And who know that when night
    Falls they will be alone,

Is moving. About that unquarried quarry,
    Over its flat north rock-face,
    White Red-Billed Tropic
    Birds slant and ride out the air
    On their paper-cutter-thin tails — quarry

Of nothing because too rare; silent —
    They swoop, balance, rise, then
    Are thrown back to their grassy cliff,
    On their own; their delicate bone-
    White tails the slimmest of fans. Silent

The path we ascend; roots like lanyards
    Or narrower, saplings give us a hand,
    And we come up into birdsong — our guide
    Long part of this jungle, we two others now
    Entering: woodspeople. Lanyard

Trees thicken, stand taller; we are right
    In the forest, tuned to each bird, to noting
    The least vibration of color
    In this deep leaf-padded green-
    Yellow strangeness; careful, we move right

Toward a courtly groaning, the Birds
     Of Paradise' showy courting; they
     Display, they let drift down that
     Underwing gossamer-fall, that
     Yellow smoke, something no other bird

Has. Then Motmots, Yellow-Tails, Jacamars, — we
     Have never seen such profusion
     Before; any branch
     Can be used by the Cocrico
     As pedestal, which he takes to; we

Have lived two whole hours alone
     On the birds' own island. We have saluted
     Them by being quiet, like sensible trees;
     By being in view, they have saluted back. The
     Birds of Paradise honored us: we saw them alone,

Perched in those thickening leaves,
     Which blur, which interrupt sight;
     Now all around us birds, rocks, trees
     Know we are going, letting them
     Be, to nest as they will in their leaves.

We have boarded our dinghy and left,
     Jounced back over
     The grey mill-wheel of water;
     Forest wisdom opens on mystery;
     Mystery roofs the shy lives we have left.

Voyage autour de ma Chambre

The Harkness Pavilion

Earliest of all rectangles,
    I see from my bed
A slab of building, grey out there,
    Then rose-dusted; then it's whacked
    By light, as the Arab
Sun hits it pell-mell. — A lateen
    Rig among shadows.

Becalmed in my bed,
    I wait out the tidal hours;
Nurses, from their corridor-jetty,
    Ferry forth and back
    Their soundless
Emollient nostrums; a silent
    Bell-buoy nudges the rocks

Which lie like cranked hospital
    Cots among shallows, teethed . . .
Beyond my bulrush bed, the eraser
    Sun rubs out buildings; over it an Arch-
    Bishop, tall in gauze mitre, white gown,
Leans. A Prophet? A Martyr?
    He looks down.

Luke, Captive

Pacing his two
Footage that way,
Rearing up, leaning this,
So that no interstice
    Would be missed, Luke
    Studied his prison-
Seminar again, on the chance . . .
The kinkajou,

Or honey-bear,
    Is a gentle, trilling,
Nocturnal creature,
Soft cinnamon-furred,
    Who would house
    If he could,
In his Central-American
Forest; Luke would

Like to.
    — What is a tree
    To an animal? A
    Direction? Camouflage?
A city-state?
    Solid in air
    It branches, and dawn
    Or noon is next door and there.

Now in his huge
    Cage, in dusky
    Day asleep, through velvet
Night he courses
    From one jungle
    To another,
In a dark sweet
Withdrawal of imagination.

Wild Geese Flying

Aware at first only of the dust of sound
  Drifting down to us here in the yard,
    I saw him look up, searching fathoms of air
      As for tidings,
        Some urgent spirits' honking aloft:
          Wild geese there — and my eyes strained after,
            Into that azure,
              Then, *there* they were: *there*,
                Flying in a straggle, so high, a wonder,
                  Glinting like wafers, silver fish-
                    Scales in the sun, a
                      Strewing of foil confetti, yet aimed;
                        The string of a kite's tail
                          Dipping, being drawn
                            Through that gulf stream of air
                              By their migrant passion; — at the edge
                              Of sight I still found them . . . .
                                Then, abruptly,
                                  Nowhere.

The Ostrich Tree — The Palm Bird

Plunging to ground, glued
To its under-earth visions, cement brows
Clamped to soil, eyes drowned, it is anchored,
A fat truncheon.

                  Why not scale that
Leaning spine, collared
Like Venus' necklace, up, up
To where a nylon
Wind feathers-over those fat
Green eggs, and branches
Swaying all round are the nest?

Again, curving toward earth,
The grey neck hurries
To stomp
Its hoof-head down deeper; the longest ostrich,
Lacklustre, an asbestos tube, is a
Message from wind to sand . . .

We can imagine climbing, monkeylike, hand-
Over-hand
To that ostrich-frond nest;
Behind it the backdrop sky just sits
Astounded at this palm bird squawking
— In total silence —
Its Creole knowledge.

Guests

Fly in for two days;
 Unpacking loud voices from
 Matching cases, they walk all the way
 To the beach, that its surf stuns,
 Then back to relax, to order rum
 Punches; — later they nibble,

Two for the barbecue:
 Packing their plates way high
 They walk tightropes toward a table,
 Waiters bowing like surf;
 Ordering everything, rum
 Consoles them. His nibbling

Old claws knick at her one or two
 Backsides; skinny as an unpacked
 Hamper, she natters, walking crane-legged
 Through the surf of chat —
 Order amounts to unpacking — then her ruffled gross
 Grosgrained vulture's neck nods to his nickety hand.

Monkey Difference

The monkey difference
   From Catholic and
      Protestant comes down to
         Most peoples' fix on guilt . . .

A maxi-skirted papacy
   Fears female more
      Than monkey; its guillotine,
         Childbed, falls on woman

Each year . . . No monkey'd be named
   Calvin: hatred of bodily
      Love is not simian, nor the
         Puritan icehouse his,

Where a dressmaker's
   Dummy can hang
      In that abbatoir
         Till the 20th child . . .

Monkey: his simon-pure,
   Active body may be
      A hieroglyph
         For life, pinpointing

It . . . In his leaf
   Cathedral he's on his own,
      Is monkey, as long as, leaping,
         Flying, he lands — and holds on.

The Lonely Pipefish

Up, up, slender
As an eel's
Child, weaving
Through water, our lonely
Pipefish seeks out his dinner,

Scanty at best; he blinks
Cut-diamond eyes — *snap* — he
Grabs morsels so small
Only a lens pinpoints them,
But he ranges all over

That plastic preserve — dorsal
Fin tremulous — *snap* — and
Another çedilla
Of brine shrimp's gone . . .
We talk on of poetry, of love,

Of grammar; he looks
At a living comma —
Snap — sizzling about
In his two-gallon Caribbean —
And grazes on umlauts for breakfast.

His pug-nosed, yellow
Mate, aproned in gloom,
Fed rarely, slumped,
Went deadwhite, as we argued on;
That rudder-fin, round as a

Pizza-cutter, at the
End of his two-inch
Fluent stick-self, lets his eyes
Pilot his mouth — *snap* . . .
Does his kind remember? Can our kind forget?

Millefleurs

For the Presentation of a Tapestry
to the Williams College Museum of Art

A wallhanging of flowers,
    Icicles, birds, teardrops,
        Lobes, animals — it hails color:

Candystriped, the barberpole
    Horn of that unicorn, whose kind red
        Eye, sharp as a javelin, is

Also appliquéd on a thicket,
    Just as are those small
        Rabbits surging

Toward safety, one of them half
    In hole. — Alas, our blue
        Stork is dying beneath a

Falcon's stabbing beak . . . One border
    Contains this whole liveliness;
        It frames nature in red . . .

In this tapestry jungle, Leo,
    With his jaunty air,
        Is no match in yellow

Mystery for the patchwork heron, —
    Half-Houdini, bodiless, his
        Bundled tail his all.

Within this limitless forest
    Of millefleurs, light
        Falls on the falcon's aimed

Beak, on the unicorn's elegant
    Duncecap, as from some infinite
        Candelabra . . . Through all these wild

Lives — posing, each in its own
    Way — regal as earth, Nature
        Deigns to sit for her portrait.

Gold *Beyond* Gold

For the Opening of the Rogers Collection of Greek Gold
at the Williams College Museum of Art

"Emeralds are green *beyond*
  Green; you look down into them
   And see the *truth* of green."

This central wreath — over
  Whose strawberry-leaves Athena's
   Heart-faced owl presides —

Is goldsmith genius, the Hellenes'
  History in art. It is a wreath-
   Symbol for Alexander, whose giant

Dream of Empire — joining
  Greece to Asia Minor — cut a swathe
   Of conquest from a route of gold.

. . . Soon, lynx, panther, griffin, ram (Darius' treasure)
  Flowered on earring, pendant,
   Belt: creatures of Dionysus, images

Of predatory urgings, fears
  Of an alloyed world,
   Alive in gold.

Herakles' knot, that amulet
  At center, frequently, of diadem,
   Thigh-band, foot-bracelet, ring,

(A reef-knot plain or garnet-studded,
    Inlaid with any treasure) — this
        Golden symbol of relationship,

They held, would heal
    Wounds; deeper than this, it stands
        For the grave, wild permanence of love.

Evening: Crown Point

Having dropped, a boiling stone,
Behind the sea, today's sun
Leaves up there a blue-black
Moiré ocean; higher,
Striations of yolk and rose; then,
Laundry-lines of silver
Strewn upon dusk.

      Into this greying
      Past, the island bats veer —
      Darting in figure-eights,
      They aquaplane on air;
      In their ballet, they skate
      Over wind-pockets, dining . . . Night
      Falls, a gavel; they have radared off.

We, on our balcony, stay on —
Above oleanders, close
To the casuarina trees which sigh
Their way to altitude. These
Grand nightfalls, splendid
As sunrise in reverse, leave us
Dark   quiet   moved . . .

Crystal-clear — Diamond-bright

As they had no ice in Tobago,
She thought it a blue shame
To see — as she cleaned up college
Rooms — all those steel-tinted ice-squares
Subsiding into drainwater. It shook her. So

She rolled tight
The rotund "cardboard-pak bag
Whose wet strength is
5½ lbs"; lugging it with
Her — baby on hip — she
Waited at the Duke Street bus-stop;
It dripped, but not much. When the bus
Hurtled up,
It clung cold to her side
Like treasure; while they stalled
In all that exhaust, she thought
About dryness in her village, Moriah,
And how only some miracle-
Magnet kept life
From falling off that

Toboggan hill. — At Main
The cool was damper. Then
Finally, out on Luck Street,
Propping open the door of
Her room — a chill still between it and her —
She was home, inside,
Alone — in a peace of crystal.

Mercedes

Hopscotch
    Through patches
    Of light, a greeneyed
Dominican slanted
    From palm-frond street-shadow in
To a job, to stay on, to be safer;
But by June, daubed soap on her mirror:
Mercedes de la Rosa está muerta

Mercedes had
    Worked Casuarina-long days:
    "San Francisco, San Francis-
    Co, San Fran . . . " written fifty-three
    Times . . . "In my grandmother's garden
Tomatoes grew, red whole
Hearts, we ate them; they said
    'Mercedes de la Rosa is dead' "

Dream-knives
    Cut out dolls — but I'll
    Help them — that leaf,
    Falling, is a dory . . .
    Chicago, Chicago;
Men: their pants
Pressed to the coil of a whip,
    Shoot billiard
    Eyes at me . . .
Merced es de la Rosa

I can hide my dolls, my
        Cuckoo-clock, though his beak
        Orders me to dance;
Sequins, I glue gold pieces, I sew
Justice on chiffon,
All colors — as I whirl,
        They dance — how my body aches!
        I must nail my cuckoo . . . The
Spinning mirror splinters:
        Mercy befits the Rose

Next day, duck with two heads,
Her radio quacked to itself; a needle
Slanted through the cuckoo's
        Heart; lint of chiffon
Rocked in Erzulie's breeze . . . "People
        Do strange sometimes," she had said,
        And,
Mercedes de la Rosa is dead

Sweet Sleep

We sleep —
After a long intractable day —
To revive, to absent
Ourselves for a bit
From responsibility ...

... But there by the road at the end of the lawn,
    Hatred flares up, violence sways
    High as the pinetrees;

    Or
    The guided tour
    Of an inner detective-
    Story pulls us on through
    Fear, crime, danger; it was all
    Known before,
    As if one were seeing something
    Already enacted: the cliff-fall,
    The revolving stairway, the moment
    When cruelty shrieked, and a whole bat-
    Gang swung at us, erasing
    Meaning ...

What has happened?
    Why should sleep
Be the rioting of a skiff
Over red water?
Without the liberty —
Haunted by narrative,
Eddying upon nothing,
Racked by symbols —
    To sleep?

The Cold Stones of the Moon

We pluck the cold stones of the moon
> With awkward grace,
> As if we were laying a floral
> Tribute before mankind;

We urge particles of these stones
> On anyone passing by,
> In the seeking gesture
> Of a blind man seeking alms;

We desire cold stones of the moon —
> Do they hum in frozen combustion? —
> As if luxe or love could be found
> In their cloudy crystal.

At Mrs. Alefounder's

Tobago

Not perched on the top of the hill
But established there, a nest
      Leaning into a blue
      Sky, this white and blue
House is an aviary; winds live outside
And in, not knowing the difference; still,

It is a house, not quite an aviary,
Though made of porches, windows,
      Weather, verandahs, open
      To all moods of air, opening
Out on trees standing apart
Like old friends . . . Save

For the one peacock, birds
Who arrive at this giant feeder
      Come in numbers. Grasping the tilt,
      Their table, they peck — swaying as the tilt
Sways — at that mash, plump
In bill. They are outdoors, but stirred

By terrace breezes . . . The stocky Anis —
Blacker than black — drive
      Roman-nosed beaks
      At their banquet, while slimmer beaks
Of Bananaquit, Woodpecker, and the dun
Or lilac Dove, or Tanagers, sky-

Blue, cloud-white partake. The Motmot's chest
Chestnut, cap azure, each delicate
     Morningcoat irridescent, one handsome
     Jewel slotting the breast; — indeed handsome
Beyond belief, at tail's end twin prongs
Support an extra feather-inch, a test

Nature has rarely passed . . . Cocricos scamper
Pheasant-heavy, purplish, a pink wattle
     As chin, body a sturdy
     Brown; for reasons of sturdy
Attraction, an undertail fan goes orange;
They loft to a plumtree and back, trample

Their provender . . . On this balcony or off
We are outside-within an aviary,
     Free in it; — then shadow
     Tucks itself underleaf, shadow
Seines birds away, ourselves also,
As night lowers over us its abrupt snuffer.

On Buccoo Reef

For Carl

Walked by these black oak
Legs, my mermaid hand held,
I drifted three feet over
Our coral kingdom — masked —
In the gentle, slow life
Of the reef.

Led by this dry hand
Through currents, edged past red
Stinging coral, growing
As men grow — goggled, I watched
The violet mandarin whiskers
Of a triggerfish,

His mustachioed tail . . .
And parrot- and squirrel-
Fish, eyes large as coins;
Others — an emerald triangle —
Wreathe rock and are gone . . .
Grizzled by sun,

My mermaid hand held,
Alive underwater, I saw,
Masked, their open eyes . . .
I am walked back now
Up in to air
By these oak legs.

AT HOME

The Blue Garden

Blue: aconite, deadly;
Iris, a grape
Hyacinth, or tulip
            Bulb lives deep
    Down under; in March
    They drill up through that frozen
            Turf. —
            Blue often reverts to magenta.

Blue: larkspur
            Sets its annual
    Poisonous
Sights at six feet; — each
Year the
            Delphinium, too,
                Kills lice;
And both revert to magenta.

Blue: the delicate fringed
            Gentian is a rarity
            To be protected,
    As gentian
    Violet is either
            Elegance or tincture;
Still, these too can revert to magenta.

Blue: cornflowers
            Secure in their August
            Field, like bachelor's
Buttons, asters — reliable
            As wheat — return
            For their violet season;
What tone is magenta?

It must be autumn's
Color: camouflage: white-
Tailed deer, red maples
Drying, that brown hawk diving
Grey as a pellet: a hodgepodge
Of pigment; middle-
Age has its own hue,
Which can easily revert to magenta.

Even so, our yarn of blood
Knits us together,
Working
Its own narrative . . .
This color may hold — blue
As some eyes are — and not
Revert, but keep cobalt, cobalt.

Otis

"When King George the Fifth
Died, my cows were happy;
They needed just that sort
Of music to ease 'em down,
          Same as a person."

Our two horses enjoy
Their separate, canopied four-
Poster stalls, with silvered
Wadding run to the ridgepole,
          That Otis made them.

"Waltzes, and something soft,
Is what cows like for music;
Then they rest quiet . . ." His sheep,
Grooming the upper pasture,
          Are belled for safety,

And their far cadence tolls
Summer's opulent hours —
While tallow fleeces thicken —
And winter's thinning days;
          "We've had a cold

Spring for eighteen years
That hasn't failed us, it's
Based on quicksand: warm
Winters, and cool in May;
          It never froze."

A wonder of nature — "wood
Splits well in cold weather" —
How things are, how things
Work, that is the study
      Of a happy man:

"Keeping animals takes
Plenty of knowing; they have
Their ways, you just must think
Quicker than they do," Otis
      Said, knowing he did.

Adam Breathing

For our Dog, Shot by Hunters

Hearing his breath, a bellows,
Fill-empty Adam's
Brown frame — he dying, perhaps,
Perhaps mending, — will air
Like a larding-needle
           Cure through him?

Listening to Adam's gospel breathing,
Raucous, impatient, while
His lungs exhort his life's
Blood to hare through the raceway
Of his body, to get on home . . .
           I wait hours

Till — hearing, quieter now,
Adam breathing, some abscess
In the heart let, some
Pegleg restored, some
Dream of the hunt expired —
           I can breathe.

Elm Burning

For Nicholas

In Zoar,
far up that hill,
Elms are burning, piled
log on log,
green, yellow,
Grey — red as a hex sign —
All sent
to their pyre, which keeps
others from sickening.
Row
On monarch
row, elms space
avenues, keep
Order in landscape, keep
the country greensilver; an elm's
Likeness is majesty; its totem
image a fountain.
Uphill
toward Zoar,
how shall our trees
be kept safe? How
Can we keep sap of our own ills
from pulsing
Bloodily as the heart?

At 79th and Park

A cry! — someone is knocked
Down on the avenue;
People don't know what to do
When a walker lies, not breathing.

I watch, 10 storeys high,
Through the acetylene air:
He has been backed up over;
Still, the accident

Is hard to credit. A group
Of 14 gathers; the Fire
Department rains like bees,
Visored, black-striped on yellow

Batting, *buzz* — they clamber
Around that globule; somebody
Brings out a comforter
For shroud; a woman's puce

Scarf bobs, from my 10th-floor view,
Desperately; by the backed truck
An arm explains, hacks air
In desperation, though no

One takes much notice. As through
A pail of glass, I see —
Far down — an ambulance,
A doctor come; they slide

Away the stretcher . . . In minutes
The piston-arm, the truck,
Puce, police, bees, group
All have been vacuumed up.

For John

    The wrecker
At last pulls in;
It sizes
Up that fossil snarled
Among weeds, hunched over
Rubble ten feet down.

    The wrecker's
Sure hands stalk his controls:
He has hooked a chain
Onto the rear axle, has a line from
Winch to farther wheel — leverage
In case that silly
Chooses
To blow on downhill,
Or slide off, a grouper,
Behind some ocean stone.

    The wrecker plays
His crane as delicately as one tunes
A harpsichord; he has heavy prey
To land; it lifts,
              lifts just
Up
   over
      weedy roadside; then he
Lets his burden
          gently
             down.

The wreck
Sprawls like a gigged
Frog in the garage, where

The wrecker,
Sculpture in his head, burls
An edifice of bright metal:
                    a perfect
Frame, in which strums his heart.

First Frost

Belatedly, I realized 1969's
First frost would change things,
Ring down a curtain of cold
To disguise our plants,

Herbs, flowers . . . Sandals
Scuffing new snow, I
Grabbed, drooped over a plastic
Bucket those vines of mini-

Tomatoes — vermillion
Spotting the snow-moth-flakes of
Our summer garden. On the laundry-
Line in the cellar, I've hung

Up, by their leaves, these white,
Green, red globules — solemn as
Kabuki dancers who bow, teeter, nod,
Awaiting a next performance.

January 26, '71

A wind-blizzard
Hurls itself screaming down,
Thieves through all corners,
Sets the old willow
To lashing itself,
Turns the grey elm's branches
To batons . . .

All our trees
Have become a febrile orchestra,
While a haze of snow speeds
Whiteness toward its barracks.

The butternut, holding up elfin
Fingers, sways, is political
On the breast of this wind;
Even a nonchalant
Bluejay zips through the
White tide with caution;

Horses are spooked — not
Knowing which side the attack
Comes from — they have windmares,
They let fly, shy, nip, buck —
Caught up in this wind-blizzard,
Forgetting the retinue
Of their day.

For Mother — A Log

On Her Eightieth Birthday
February 11, 1968

At twenty:
    A girl, sun-turned,
        Drove and knew horses,
    Understood collie pups, and had
    Learned what the loss of her
        Father meant.

At forty:
    A skipper, married,
        She held fast to the tiller
    Over undertows; she and Daddy
    Loved children: she
        Brought us together.

At sixty:
    A woman: Daddy,
        The anchor, gone, she
    Caulked the whole family, cared for
    All grandchildren, ran
        A tight ship.

At eighty:
    A great lady, warm
        In the sun; thyme
    Her perfume, nature her familiar
    Spirit; her life alive;
        We honor and love her.

Best of Show

Wheatfields of chiffon,
Afghans are blown
Into the ring: spunsilk
Waterfall, while

Popeyed Chihuahuas
Toothpick about, each
Radar-cocked ear
Plucking news . . . Now

Golden as carp,
Pekinese waddling
On fins of fur,
Whelk tails, swim in;

Next, the Great Danes,
Brindle or pinto,
Sleek as wallpaper,
Enter

Before feathered
English
Setters, time on their
Point to snoot

Most poodles, those
Peacock, tonsured, bright-
Eyed balls of cotton-
Candy; and

Bassetts,
Paws whiter than sneakers,
Map ears their
Epaulettes; or

Weimaraners,
Coats silver
On bacon, yellow
Eyes sly; so different

From Huskies',
Whose Arctic
Look is a squint . . .
These breeds strut till,

Wheezing over its bow-
Legs, a lap
Dog trembles in:
Best of show!

Focus

Through the storm windows' double
Pane, our horses wander blurred
Like forms shivered out of old
Dice-cups. Vision flutters;
      It simmers like chestnuts
      Smoking over
Winter coals; blurred.

A shift of focus leads
To where fear starts up like decibels,
Clanging, roaring;
      Where the imagination
Skins into dark troughs, punctured
      By feared sound.
Inside the brain-pan, bells

Ring quiet away. Medically
One is not safe — the small
Cranium dwindles, almost no
Light gets in. It is as if a coconut
Shrank on itself to a golfball,
While the rioting
Of experience keeps pumping on all

Pistons: felt, understood, argued.
But later, nothing was there ... Memory held
No more than a pin-prick, glaze
Of nothing, patting the featherbed
Into which one must have fallen
When the mind cut out light.
To the trepanned head, told

That focus will return, the shutter
Open, letting light in, that memory
Will snap back to the Judge's seat,
Condemning darkness . . . It may . . . Or
Perhaps, like a wizened
Head it will end up on Sixth Avenue,
Mincing in the breeze.

So, out of focus — ragged
Dreams, phrases — winking dull
On and off — 414-317 —
Memory chutes alongside
Happenings — disappears . . . returns . . .
Consciousness is a full
Or empty skull or grail.

Threesquare at the Landfill

Trotting, the ancient man,
like a kind kobold, veers
to help me, while Callaghan,
    bluff as a mesa,

takes his time, leans
a strong hand over the broken
tailgate, reaches out all that green
    plastic trove, detritus

of living, bits of tame
rubble for future lawns;
meanwhile our brown dog, Adam,
    circumnavigates new territory . . .

This town dump, this Grand
Pownal Canyon, whose fortress-
nature's 'dozed from sand,
    is theatre for this trio:

Adam sniffing; Callaghan
playing the real Callaghan;
Adam pausing; the old man
    being a very old man.

Talking to Animals

For Cary

When there are animals about, who else —
People aside — does one talk to?
They form an environment of ear and eye
Most finely adjusted to turns
Of mood: terror, humor . . .

The domesticated: cats and dogs
Speak freely, handle their own
Lives, adjust our natures
To theirs and back; as cattle —
Those enormous oblongs of good-

Will — did they state their strength,
Could smash a barn a day;
As ducks in their sewing circle
Wonder, wander, flapping their
Fluent tails; as a mare

Lumbers, an iron horse on the turntable,
Setting forth a fact, while her foal's eyes dance
Like legs. Smaller creatures: four
Inches of chipmunk tell hazard
From ruin as people can't . . .

Making oneself understood
To animals — as to people —
Is a question of tone of voice,
Of communication just
Right for that neighbor;

Perhaps of being inside
A hogan, or in the middle
Of anywhere, one's antennae out,
Like my Beaver-Spirit who takes — deep
In his Eskimo ear — much wisdom from a Loon.

Shell

The strong delicate shell
    Of the body — shoulders
    Rising like music, subsiding,
Turning toward me like dawn —
    Arches, in warmth, a wave
    Fluted, and I rise up
To welcome the wash of the sea.

A small kettledrum, nacre,
    The slim clear heart-of-pearl
    That relays the
Ocean's tidal message,
    Meanwhile it secretes,
    As flesh does, rainbows — holds dawn in its
Curve — yet bears them within.

All these ivory breezes
    Indent the sea; and sea
    And wind thus form
A shell, or a vast scallop
    Of air and water; they meet
    Forming each other.
Shell warms; when warmed

It emerges from its resonant
    Depth, draws one to look
    Down to the whorled
Architecture of the human. Warmth is
    Kindled by touch. Into
    This scalloped world we are born:
Ourselves shaped by our white housing of skin.

August

Thinking of insight,
I notice swallows
Teetering over the wire,
About to migrate;

Aware of instinct
Swaying like morning-glories
Deep-blue up there, I question
Those who lack all

Capacity for feeling,
Can't act in concert:
To fly off — ? To stay — ?
Flooded again

With knowledge
Of love happening, held
Onto — , transparent
With this,

I hang my life
On the brown hooks of my shoulders,
As one who comes to a well
And carries so much away.

Notes for a Foghorn

Long — short —
    Smothered
        By air
            That sound

Awls
    Through a thick
        Mist; as a hoarse
            His Master's

Voice
    Would megaphone,
        Barking
            About reefs; or a

Cowhorn — Europa
    Lowing in minor
        Key, dog-paddling,
            Lost . . . As from

A cornucopia
    Of danger, Poseidon
        Roars, brandishes tides,
        The sea his cloak.

Ouroborus

With age, mind
Watches that intestinal tree: —
Throat, lung, kidney

And so forth, while I
Eat crystals
And they disappear;

The inside worm
Seeks down its inner
Telescope, chuting

Toward where heart —
All its vivid feathers
Dull now — takes

Its own pulse, wonders
How much the frail
Casing of the bowel

Can stand today;
Thought chutes, pulling
Itself after itself,

Yet opts: I live, I
Consume myself,
I die.

For an Old Friend

HFZ at 90

At peace on your porch —
    The garden
    Smouldering under the dark
    Vigil of cypress and privet —

You tell me that,
    Free now
    From desire and surfeit, you
    Can see human emotion in scale:

An Alpine relief
    Map,
    Rainbow geometry, bells
    Lunging in the Campanile . . . .

This hullabaloo
    About life
    Is not my forte, you might
    Add, as I ask your blessing. . . .

Brushstrokes, this green
    Wisdom,
    A vine: sitting frail in your chair,
    Towering, dispensing light.

Jim

Sat there
In a folding chair
Awaiting his father:

Sixteen
Is young, if it means
Only more beatings,

Or older
When the boy was ordered
Monthlong to his room last year —

That June crept
By in exploding slow-motion; he erupted
July 1st, like a puppy

Ran each four corners
Of the yard, while his mother's
Eyes were grey with tears . . .

Then last week his father loomed
In the doorway: — so framed,
He was shot four times;

Sound
Catapulted against the background
Hill, the slag-dark ground,

To ricochet
From that squat tannery
Which was the future.

This much older
Boy, is he in second child-
Hood now? Can he recall

More than that he sat there
In a folding chair
Waiting for his father?

Still-life: New England

From that old cow in the field
  A calf was born;
He struggles now to rise —
  No, he cannot
Yet, on his tapestry legs;
  The cow, crosshatched
With dirt, lice, underfed,
  Her cud a sour
Lozenge in her throat
  Rolls agate eyes.

Sheep with their earnest profiles
  Vaguely pit
Their muzzles at the gate,
  Wait to stampede;
If luck works for them, bars
  Will slide by their neat
Feet; grass will surround
  Them, camouflage
Through which they'll crop a path
  All through green summer.

While the boar, in the strawyard
  Of his excrement,
Tunnels, grunting through
  Each four-walled day,
The cow lies in the field;
  The calf she bore
Dies — . With what a spray
  Of whiskers, the yellow
Barncat saunters forth,
  Smells death, returns,

Prinks in the barndoorway . . .
           The cow lurches
To her feet, in need of fodder,
           Hocks trembling,
Ridgepole of hipbones slanting
           Through her canvas hide
Sharp as a longhorn's skull;
           She subsides —
Her eyes, agate no longer,
           Thicken to rubber.

48044

A Drachma for Myself

We have in hand
A precious coin, whose two
Sides understanding

May put together:
A jackal runs a deer
Which, caught in silver,

Begs, beseeches,
But is not freed nor spared
His savaging;

Which melts in fear
As if minted to symbolize
The face of terror . . .

On the other side
Of the coin the victim outstrips
Every living thing,

Leaves behind all
Connection: love, kin —
In her crisis of running

Becoming as ruthless
A creature as any the wilderness
Has seen; so out

Of relation to all
But the tyranny of her fear . . .
Grieve for this runner

Who flees on both sides
Of how rare a coin, so
Piteously, so wildly!

Cardinal

With deep snow
    A fresh page
        Stretches
        Toward the tree-
    Line; within, a new page
Reflects the grey-white of

Ceiling; never flat,
    Snow rolls with the
        Earth's breathing —
        Slivers
    Of light, reflected,
Skate like grasshoppers

Over the whole white-
    Carpeted landscape,
        Or again, in grey
        Weather, blend into
    Dusk; — those matchstick
Trees out there, poled

Into snow, are characters
    Cutting their own shadow. My
        Page now has markings:
        Hieroglyphs of
    Talon, pen, shade,
Hoof range over this open

Country, imprint it. On snow-
   Fall — as the white
      Magic between us
     Is signed — I see
   The cardinal's red cursive
Line, written on winter, writing to spring . . .